Honoring the
FIRST LADY
of Your Ministry

Yolanda Gilliam

Copyright © 2017 by Yolanda Gilliam
Los Angeles, California
All rights reserved
Printed and Bound in the United States of America

Published And Distributed By
Gilliam Publishing House
Los Angeles, California
perfectedwoman@hotmail.com

Packaging/Consulting
Professional Publishing House
1425 W. Manchester Ave. Ste. B
Los Angeles, California 90047
323-750-3592
Email: professionalpublishinghouse@yahoo.com
www.Professionalpublishinghouse.com

Cover design: TWA Solutions.com
First printing October 2017
978-0-9994927-0-3
10987654321

No part of this book may be reproduced, stored in a retrieval system or transmitted in any form or by any means without the prior written permission of the publisher—except by a reviewer who may quote brief passages in a review to be printed in a newspaper, magazine or journal.

Table of Contents

Dedication 5

Introduction 7

The Origination of the Term: First Lady 9

Protecting the First Lady of Your Ministry 15

The Royal Court 19

Which First Lady Are You? 27

Proverbs 31 Woman 35

    ❦ A Rare Beauty 38

    ❦ Business Woman 39

    ❦ Character, Grace, and Beauty 42

A Living Testimony 47

Sarah *vs.* Hagar 51

Conclusion 57

References 59

About the Author 61

Dedication

I give honor to my Lord and Savior Jesus Christ for allowing me to write this book to encourage First Ladies around the world that they are special, loved, and appreciated.

To the women of God, I hope you can learn and apply the encouragement in being a God-fearing Proverbs 31 Woman.

To my mom, the spiritual pillar and foundation of love, hope, and wisdom you have instilled in me. I praise God for your example and your never-giving-up attitude.

To my best friends and awesome brothers: James, Carl, and Joshua. Thank you, James, for supporting and listening to me. Carl, you never allow the rain to fall on your sunshine.

Thank you for being there for me and supporting my endeavors. Joshua, thank you for the inspirational quotes and songs you give to me. I love you guys.

To my son, Michael, who has become a wonderful and talented man. You are a blessing to me. I am proud of you and I love you!

To my cousins Christina and Jessica for helping me proofread this book a million times. Thank you for your suggestions and being there every step of the way. Thank you, Sister Lilly, for praying for me and speaking success into my life. Love you guys!

Pastor David W. Cross and First Lady Jacqueline Cross, you are a blessing to me. Thank you for believing in me. Love you both!

Introduction

The First Lady is a reflection of our Lord and Savior Jesus Christ. Surrender, prayer, fasting, compassion, discipline, and spiritual support for the body of Christ surround her role as First Lady. Her duties of giving herself sacrificially in ministry are enormous, but a call God has placed on her life to be a blessing to his people.

The First Lady exhibits righteous characteristics displayed by meekness and poise. She embraces the honor of being a Proverbs 31 woman without any hesitation or resistance. *Honoring the First Lady of Your Ministry* will teach Bible believers the importance of lifting their First Lady up in prayer, the importance of her position, and applying the spiritual tools needed to assist her in ministry.

Our reverence, respect, and honor for the First Lady should be present at all times. I encourage every believer to apply principles of prayer, fasting, encouragement, and protection for our leadership. These foundational principles are the spiritual building blocks our First Lady needs to help strengthen her. The body of Christ should set aside daily devotional prayers that speak life over the life of our First Lady.

I can't stress the importance of a believer's role of protecting the First Lady's anointing by being a faithful, spiritual support beam. We are the spiritual secret service agents for our First Lady. She needs us and we need her. Let's back her up by being a dedicated ministry who strives for her well-being based on God's Word.

Enjoy!

The Origination of the Term: First Lady

Termed in the late 1800s, First Lady referred to a woman who was married or assisted the President of the United States. Some wives of the president did not want the title of First Lady because they felt the role was overwhelming or ridiculous. In such cases, when the wives of presidents weren't in favor of exercising the role of First Lady, a relative or close friend assumed it. It wasn't until 1934 that the term First Lady became officially recognized. There is no record in determining when the church began using the term First Lady, but many Christian churches use the title of First Lady. In today's modern times, the wives of dignitaries, leaders of countries, and ministers of the church graciously accept the term. In addition, the First Lady has taken an active role in spreading the message of hope, encouraging collegiate education, and bringing awareness about health and political issues that affect mankind. The First Lady continues to be the backbone to their husband, families, ministries, and nation.

Merriam-Webster defines First Lady as [1]*the wife, hostess, female friend or relative of the chief executive of a country, state or city.* [2]*The first woman of a specified profession or art.*

The Bible (KJV) defines First Lady as the *wife of a bishop or pastor of a ministry. A wife who assists her husband through prayer, comfort and encouragement. A woman who is grave, not slanders, sober, faithful in all things* (1 Timothy 3:11). *A woman who behaves as becometh holiness, not false accusers, not given to much wine, teachers of good things, teaching young women to be sober, to love their husbands, to love their children, to be discreet, chaste, keepers at home,*

The Origination of the Term: First Lady

good, obedient to their own husbands, that the Word of God be not blasphemed (Titus 2:3-5).

The First Lady is quick to listen and slow to speak, assisting her husband through the wisdom and guidance of the Holy Spirit. She has a life built on the Word of God and instilled principles of righteous living. She studies her Heavenly Father's behavior to ensure she mimics him and displays a life serving His purpose. She does not partake in negative living that would cause blemishes in her Christian walk with Christ. She is always pursuing a relationship with Jesus and desires to share her testimony with the body of Christ to encourage them to be righteous overcomers. Those who aspire to live a life pleasing to the Lord desire her lifestyle. Her husband, children, and individuals surrounding her life greatly appreciate her. She practices the principles of God first, then family. She doesn't put her career, church, or organizations before the cares of her family because she knows that God entrusted her to assist them in the things of God. She honors her husband by listening to him, caring for him, and being attentive to what's important to him. She is not intoxicated with television shows or literature that does not edify her walk with Christ. She is careful not to participate in idle gossip or take on habits that would threaten or strip away her anointing and relationship with others. She strives to be last and not first. She is always putting the needs of others before herself, but careful to use wisdom to ensure she is not compromising her Christianity or calling to the ministry. She desires to please the Lord and those around her. She carries herself as an ambassador, representing her Heavenly Father through her way of speaking, disposition, attire, and truth of God's Word.

After carefully examining the term First Lady, I have concluded that a First Lady is never born but developed. She is the pinnacle point of the existence of mankind. She is the royal ambassador of God's kingdom and clothes herself in elegance. The definitions of *ambassador* and *royalty* are as follows:

- *Ambassador*: A minister of the highest rank sent to a foreign court to represent there his sovereign or country. Ambassadors are either ordinary [or resident] or extraordinary, that is, sent upon some special or unusual occasion or errand. An official messenger and representative.

- ***Royalty***: the authority of a monarch, which includes families and having the right to exercise rank, status, power, and authority.

As an ambassador, the First Lady represents God, husband, children, and church family. As a representative of these capacities, she is often misunderstood and perceived as a perfect, flawless individual who holds a prestigious title. In fact, she is a human being who does her best to be the anchor that assist, direct, lead, and counsel through the help of the Holy Spirit.

The First Lady is a unique individual who carefully seeks God's wisdom for her life and the lives of others. Whether you're a wife, mother, aunt, businesswoman, grandmother you represent your Heavenly Father's royal court as His ambassador. You create destiny, good or bad. What type of destiny are you creating?

As women who represent our Heavenly Father, it is important to remember that our marriage to Him will reflect our marriage to our spouse and relationship with others. Do you reflect and represent your Heavenly Father's kingdom through your lifestyle?

PROTECTING THE FIRST LADY OF YOUR MINISTRY

The essential components of protecting your leaders are prayer, fasting, and positioning yourself as a spiritual support beam. The First Lady experiences challenges, disappointments, and emotional roller coasters of life just like anyone else. Because the body of Christ tends to see her position as glamorous or prestigious, we sometimes forget that she is human with real life issues.

God made people to praise and worship Him. Above all else, He wanted company. Made in His image, we desire to be loved, appreciated, and wanted. The First Lady is no different. She needs us and we need her. God uniquely made us and there is no one else in existence like us. Just think, we look just like God, but acting like God is another thing! God placed us in our First Ladies' lives to help, befriend, and appreciate them.

The First Lady needs support, prayer, and fellowship from her ministry. As women, we combat many emotions that generate from life. Some of the major issues are family, health, job, and people we interact with daily. Regardless of the issues of life, it's important that the First Lady consult with someone she can trust when things seem to be overwhelming.

Queen Esther was a woman honored by her husband the king, royal dignitaries, and women of her royal court. She showed humility, reverence and, most importantly, she worshipped God. She took her position seriously, without pride or reservation. When trouble arose, she sought wisdom and sound instruction from those she trusted. Her decision to take a stand could help her people or cause them to die a gruesome death. Can you imagine how much pressure was on her? Although the mountain seemed enormous, the wisdom and faith she needed caused her to lean on her Heavenly Father for help. She called her Jewish people and women of her royal court to fast and pray for God's mercy for three days and three nights because of unfortunate circumstances surrounding her and the people she loved. She needed support from everyone to help her through this tough time. The women of her royal court had compassion on their queen and came to a mutual, spiritual agreement to support her through prayer. They could have complained and eaten a cookie, but they chose to support her with a sincere heart. That's favor!

The First Lady needs concrete support, knowing someone is in her corner. Sometimes she feels alone, distracted and overwhelmed. God placed us in her life to listen, give advice, and extend a helping hand. She needs the right support and guidance. We are designed to help lighten her load, not add to it. We are burden busters!

We need to help assist our First Lady by embracing a teachable spirit, being readily available, maintaining a spirit of prayer, fasting and being a friend who can be trusted. Be reminded that our First Lady takes on many different roles that require time, attention, and work! With this comes enormous responsibility.

THE ROYAL COURT

Many First Ladies have established women's fellowship meetings, conferences and retreats that help build and inspire the people of God, physically and spiritually. These special events require careful planning by the First Lady and teams of individuals who help ensure these events are well planned and organized. These teams of individuals represent the First Lady's royal court and are sensitive to the needs of her vision God has instilled inside her. In addition, they help the First Lady focus on being effective in ministry by taking the responsibility of caring for her physical and spiritual needs. The women who help the First Lady accomplish the vision God has placed inside her and are the royal court of armor bearers called to specific duties.

The royal court consists of five categories of women who help execute the vision of the First Lady: Chamberlin Women, Women of Worship & Praise, Women of Intercession, Women of Service and Women of Wisdom.

- **Chamberlin Women** are the chief leaders responsible for managing the royal court and executing duties delegated by the First Lady. They are second in command with exclusive rights to make decisions that would reflect the orders of the First Lady. They strive to reflect the godly attributes of the First Lady and put her needs above her their own. Their attire is unique, uniformed and distinguishes royal elegance. Their position is God-ordained and taken seriously. They are friends of the First Lady, and they take an active role to ensure the protection and reverence of the First Lady. They surround the First Lady with a spirit of intercession of prayer and fasting. They represent the First Lady when she's not present at events and they strive not to participate in ungodly conversation or activities. They consume themselves in holiness and read their Bibles every day to build their relationship with God. They are women of strength, honor, and dependability.

- The sole focus of the **Women of Worship & Praise** is to give honor to God through song. In ministry, they sing songs that bring healing, deliverance, salvation, and reverence to our Heavenly Father. Women of Worship & Praise sing songs that reflect oneness with God and the First Lady's biblical message. Every song sang expresses a fulfillment of being one with Christ. These women strive to be one with God, the First Lady, and each other. They desire to please God through their sound of worship and praise. Daily devotion, prayer, fasting, and practice are priorities for these women. They believe excellence is not an option but a way of life. They bring forth a harmonious anointing because they endeavor to be unified and they have a desire to want others to do the same.

- Twenty-four **Women of Intercession** pray twenty-four hours a day for twenty-four components of the First Lady's life. These components are: health, finances, family, spending time in the Word of God, vision, relationship with God, spiritual gifts, ministry, desires, needs, vacations, home, neighborhood, transportation, friends, mind, speech, rest, attitude, ministry helpers, happiness, favor, healing and women God has placed in her life to help her fulfill the vision God has given her. Women of Intercession are assigned one of the components and pray every day for an hour about that component in her life. They are the spiritual call center to the First Lady. Women of Intercession provide local and long distance spiritual assistance and keep her petitions confidential. These women are prayer warriors who pray against distractions or obstacles the First Lady may face or experience. They are the emergency spiritual team that helps enforce peace within the royal court and shuts down the devil's devices of discord and confusion. Women of Intercession are Bible believers, putting God first, readers, and doers of the Word of God, maintaining a consistent life of surrender, fasting, and prayer. These women pray the First Lady makes the right decisions concerning the ministry, and spiritual and physical development.

- ***Women of Service*** are called to work, produce results of excellence, and lead others by their example. They sincerely serve without expecting accolades, payments, or rewards for service rendered. They understand their attitude of service must reflect the attitude of our Heavenly Father and First Lady. Women of Service express themselves as kind, friendly, joyful people who pride themselves in making others feel warm and welcome. They are adamant about serving God's people and know that God carefully selected them to render a service of homage. Their duties include: greeting God's people, collecting offering, clean and prepare the house of God, count people in the service, provide a summary of the service in weekly meetings, distributing and collecting surveys to better service the people, distribute bulletins, collect details of visitors to allow for structure, follow-up and display a key quality of humility. They strive to be on time and always arrive earlier than the rest of the congregation. They know that their area of service is not only to help assist the First Lady, but it's a way of life. They are women of prayer, fasters, tithers, and conscious of the needs of the First Lady. Lastly, they are the door/gatekeepers of the ministry. They are the eyes of the service. Their position is to watch and pray against anything that is not right in the service. They surround themselves with peace and unification to ensure their spirits line up with the Word of God and their First Lady.

- ***Women of Wisdom*** rightly divide God's Word to help the First Lady make wise choices in matters concerning the women God has placed in the ministry. They are careful to listen first and answer last. They are sensitive to hearing the voice of God and strive to please God. They read their Bible's every day to hear the voice of God. They provide knowledge, understanding, and experience when giving advice to the First Lady. They have a sincere desire to lead their First Lady and the ministry in the right direction. They provide the ability to tell the difference between right and wrong.

As the body of Christ, our goal is to pray about the position we are called to hold in the royal court. Which royal court are you a part of?

WHICH FIRST LADY ARE YOU?

First Lady Esther
(Splendid Galaxy)

A woman whose outer and inner beauty reflects the character of Christ, she seeks to please God and her royal court. Her life is surrender, prayer, and fasting. She values her husband, family, and royal court. She gives gifts and words of appreciation. She displays her obedience to God through her godly actions and her personality shines brightly. She strives to make peace and not war.

First Lady Claudia
(Encourager)

Her words of inspiration are magnified and digested as rich vitamins and fruits. Her daily dose of encouragement is given to spiritually build her brother and sisters in the Lord. She speaks, reads, and lives God's Word every day. She doesn't allow the negative circumstances to cloud what the Word of God says. She doesn't take her position lightly and uses it to glorify her Heavenly Father.

First Lady Anna
(Favor or Grace): 'She waited to see Jesus' belief in God

She believes that *'faith is the substance of things hoped for and the evidence of things not seen'* (Hebrews 11:1). Whether she is praying or believing God for something or someone, she believes through prayer that it will come to pass. She doesn't allow the devil's darts to steer her in the wrong direction. She exercises her faith daily through example and her way of life. She consistently receives God's favor because she never doubts that He will fulfill His word and answer her prayers. She stands in the gap for others who trust her with their petitions. She is God's prayer bullet, faith builder, and entrusted servant.

First Lady Naomi
(My Joy, Pleasantness of Jehovah)

Although discouragement may come from the left and right, she never stops trusting God. She strives to teach God's ways and what pleases Him. She doesn't allow the situations of life to deter her from the blessings of God. She understands that her God is the God of plenty and more than enough. Every time she looks around, God is blessing her from the east, west, north, and south. She is a giver of too much! Her root of trusting and believing in God is so deeply planted that her strong belief in God is greatly contagious. She is walking in faith.

First Lady Ruth (Female Friend/Friend of God)

She thirsts to be like God, to please and honor Him. Everywhere she turns, she ends up on Favor Avenue, Favor Street, Favor Boulevard, and Favor Place. She carries herself with honor, confidence, and peace. She doesn't allow where she came from to dictate her future, nor does she allow the devil to remind her of her past. Instead, she uses her past as a pulpit to relate to others who have experienced the bondage of darkness and shine the floodlight of God's Word over their lives to be delivered and set free. She is humble with her brothers and sisters and a destroyer of the kingdom of darkness. She is always making provisions to help others before she helps herself. All who make contact with her honor and love her. She is not only a friend of God, but also a friend to others.

First Lady Sarah
(Captain, Commander, Mother of Many Nations)

She knows who she is, where she comes from, and where she is going. Her ways are God's ways, her speech is God's speech, and her thoughts are God's thoughts. Created to help and birth nations, she understands that she cannot allow anything to hinder her anointing. She leads in humility, she walks with authority, and she moves with grace. She duplicates herself in the lives of others, ensuring the duplication is built on the Word of God. When she seeks the face of God, He is consistently reminding her that she is His reflection, His voice and His servant. She is called to build and equip God's people for ministry.

First Lady Deborah
(means *bee*—to swarm around God and the sting of a *bee* represents God's Word that's used to perfect us; Prophetess, Leader and Judge)

She is sensitive to the voice of God and leads with boldness. She understands her calling is not a desirable one, but she accepts the outcomes, knowing all things work together for the good, to those who love God. She is a discerner and qualified by God to make decisions on His behalf. Her love for God's people is tremendously seen through her walk with Him and she is a living example of strength and honor. Lastly, she doesn't take for granted the decisions she makes through the leading of the Holy Spirit, words of wisdom she imparts because these things will not only impact her but a nation.

Whether your First Lady is a prayer warrior, encourager, ministry builder, or teacher, she is called to render service to God and to others. There are so many examples in the Word of God that talks about godly women stepping up to build the people of God. The foundation of God's Word was built on the principles of family. Each component in the family is needed to help birth a nation. We should be so ecstatic to be a part of God's plan. It is so imperative that the First Lady understands that not only is her example watched, but appreciated. Like a minister I heard years ago say, "Don't worry about the few that dislike you, but concentrate on the hundreds that love you."

Your example is so important to the body of Christ. Be encouraged to find yourself as one of the First Ladies you previously read about and in an example, you see in another. Be sure the individual you're observing is first God-driven! Being an example is not easy, but it will eventually be rewarding. Remember to duplicate yourself in the life of another every day. Ask yourself, "Since receiving Christ as my Lord and Savior, would God be pleased with the person I've become today?"

PROVERBS 31 WOMAN

Proverbs 31:10-31 is one of the most powerful verses in the Bible, referencing the attributes of a woman whose virtuous character continues to impact nations. Its foundation is the platform and heartbeat of who a woman of God desires to become.

Proverbs 31:10-31:

10 [a]Who can find a virtuous and capable wife?
She is more precious than rubies.
11 Her husband can trust her,
and she will greatly enrich his life.

¹² She brings him good, not harm,
  all the days of her life.
¹³ She finds wool and flax
  and busily spins it.
¹⁴ She is like a merchant's ship,
  bringing her food from afar.
¹⁵ She gets up before dawn to prepare breakfast
  for her household
  and plan the day's work for her servant girls.
¹⁶ She goes to inspect a field and buys it;
  with her earnings she plants a vineyard.
¹⁷ She is energetic and strong,
  a hard worker.
¹⁸ She makes sure her dealings are profitable;
  her lamp burns late into the night.
¹⁹ Her hands are busy spinning thread,
  her fingers twisting fiber.
²⁰ She extends a helping hand to the poor
  and opens her arms to the needy.
²¹ She has no fear of winter for her household,
  for everyone has warm[b] clothes.

Proverbs 31 Woman

²² She makes her own bedspreads.
She dresses in fine linen and purple gowns.
²³ Her husband is well known at the city gates,
where he sits with the other civic leaders.
²⁴ She makes belted linen garments
and sashes to sell to the merchants.
²⁵ She is clothed with strength and dignity,
and she laughs without fear of the future.
²⁶ When she speaks, her words are wise,
and she gives instructions with kindness.
²⁷ She carefully watches everything in her household
and suffers nothing from laziness.
²⁸ Her children stand and bless her.
Her husband praises her:
²⁹ "There are many virtuous and capable women in the world,
but you surpass them all!"
³⁰ Charm is deceptive, and beauty does not last;
but a woman who fears the LORD will be greatly praised.

³¹ Reward her for all she has done.
Let her deeds publicly declare her praise.

A Rare Beauty
Proverbs 31: 10-12

¹⁰ [a]Who can find a virtuous and capable wife?
She is more precious than rubies.
¹¹ Her husband can trust her,
and she will greatly enrich his life.
¹² She brings him good, not harm,
all the days of her life.

The Proverbs 31 Woman is a genuine, trustworthy, law-abiding, decent, ethical, honorable, respectable, noble, blameless woman whose mere motives are to motivate, encourage, and uplift someone other than herself. She is a rare beauty. She deposits seeds of faith, love, hope, and biblical principles in her husband's life. She honors him and gives him good things his whole life and never evil. The virtuous woman protects her husband through a prayer and fasted lifestyle. Her husband doesn't worry about his everyday needs because he knows his wife will take care of it. He is confident and relies on his wife to help him make decisions that will affect him, her, and the household. She asks the Holy Spirit for daily guidance to discern the good and bad to help her make the right decisions to assist her husband. She brings her husband value and he's proud she's his wife.

Business Woman
(Home and Work)

Proverbs 31: 13-24
¹³ She finds wool and flax
and busily spins it.
¹⁴ She is like a merchant's ship,
bringing her food from afar.
¹⁵ She gets up before dawn to prepare breakfast for her household

and plan the day's work for her servant girls.
¹⁶ She goes to inspect a field and buys it;
with her earnings she plants a vineyard.
¹⁷ She is energetic and strong,
a hard worker.
¹⁸ She makes sure her dealings are profitable;
her lamp burns late into the night.
¹⁹ Her hands are busy spinning thread,
her fingers twisting fiber.
²⁰ She extends a helping hand to the poor
and opens her arms to the needy.
²¹ She has no fear of winter for her household,
for everyone has warm[b] clothes.
²² She makes her own bedspreads.
She dresses in fine linen and purple gowns.
²³ Her husband is well known at the city gates,
where he sits with the other civic leaders.
²⁴ She makes belted linen garments
and sashes to sell to the merchants.

Proverbs 31 Woman

The virtuous woman is a businesswoman. Described as a merchant ship, constantly negotiating and building new business relationships to help add additional income to the household, she has wealth and believes in buying the best of everything. She buys food from faraway places, ensuring her household eats only the best dishes. This woman is not playing!

She gets up early before her servants, prepares the household and itinerary for the day. She is organized, writes the vision out, and makes it plain. The Proverbs 31 Woman is a real estate investor. She takes the money she has earned from making clothes and merchant ship negotiations and invests in the land to make more money for her household. She takes her vitamins, exercises, and eats healthy to keep making the right business decisions. All her dealings bring a good return on investments. She works late at night, making clothes and meeting the demand of her customers.

The Proverbs 31 Woman's husband is a dignitary and well known throughout the city. He has relationships with other officials. Because of his status, the virtuous woman represents her husband's reputation and household with godly character and integrity. She welcomes and helps those in need with great compassion. She doesn't fear the winter because she has made accommodations. Therefore, she has saved up money, the pantry is filled with food, made quilts to keep the family and staff warm, and made enough merchandise to continue making money for the household in the winter.

Character, Grace, and Beauty
Proverbs 31: 25-31

[25] She is clothed with strength and dignity,
and she laughs without fear of the future.
[26] When she speaks, her words are wise,
and she gives instructions with kindness.
[27] She carefully watches everything in her household
and suffers nothing from laziness.
[28] Her children stand and bless her.
Her husband praises her:

²⁹ "There are many virtuous and capable women
in the world,
but you surpass them all!"
³⁰ Charm is deceptive, and beauty does not last;
but a woman who fears the Lord will be
greatly praised.
³¹ Reward her for all she has done.
Let her deeds publicly declare her praise.

The Proverbs 31 Woman's character is displayed by courage and self-respect. She is a planner and doer. When she speaks, it's meaningful and she directs with understanding. She tends to the needs of her house and doesn't procrastinate. Her children admire her and her husband compliments her. There are many upstanding and intelligent women in the world, but the Proverbs 31 Woman bypasses all of them. Cunningness is misleading and good looks do not last, but a woman who respects the Lord will be greatly honored.

Let's Recap!

A woman of God has integrity, grace, and a wealth of knowledge. She is an entrepreneur, despises procrastination, meticulously plans and executes. In addition, she wakes up before the sun rises, prepares breakfast for her family and writes out the schedule for her employees. She is a real estate investor. She educates herself about the investment she is planning to purchase before she buys it. She ensures it's a business deal that will yield a rate of return. A woman of God uses her money to purchase what she needs for her business, being sensitive not to use her husband's income that takes care of the household. She is full of energy, life, strong, and works hard. Her investments allow her to buy the best. She keeps her credit history in good condition and doesn't overspend. Overspending and not being credit conscious reflects irresponsibility and carelessness. A woman of God is constantly creating new ideas. She has a nonprofit to give back to those in need. She is wealthy and able to give money to the poor.

She steers the ship in her home and makes sure it's on the right course. She is slow to speak and quick to listen. She attentively listens to God's voice everywhere she sits, stands, sleeps, and walks (Psalm 1). She's not lazy and refuses to embrace its character. All who know her admonishes her accomplishments and humbling spirit. She doesn't have to be cunning, beautiful, or seductive to gain things or people's respect. Her character displays the fruit of the spirit and speaks for itself (Galatians 5:22). It's priceless and can't be bought.

Can we find the Proverbs 31 Woman in someone or ourselves? That is a tall order, but ladies, that's who God says we should be; spiritual architects constantly developing character in ourselves and others. If God put a question mark (Who can find a virtuous woman?), He's probably still looking for her. The Bible says if you find her, the price for her is far above rubies. The ruby is the most expensive gemstone in the world. Its value is above diamonds. A rare, unique gemstone, that when found, is cherished and priceless.

Women, there is no price on our value, it's priceless. We are unique individuals and made in God's image. It's easy to identify a virtuous woman because she stands out amongst the crowd. She doesn't go where others go, do what others do, or say what others say.

Unlock your virtuous destiny today by being that Proverbs 31 Woman. The Proverbs 31 Woman built a legacy that impacted those around her and it continues to affect us today. Build a legacy that will impact those around you and the world.

The virtuous woman is peculiar, always including God in every decision. She strives for righteousness in every area of her life and turns away from anything not right. The virtuous woman's ultimate goal is to please God and seek His wisdom every day.

Lastly, you find a virtuous woman through the Holy Spirit and not through physical eyes. God will only unveil her to those deserving of her. She is extraordinary and women like her are scarce.

A Living Testimony

I've watched many poised and courageous women in my life. It's not only the obstacles I've observed them endure, but also, more importantly, how they went through a tough time not knowing how they would get through it.

Of the women in my life, my mom is a Proverbs 31 Woman. I've seen my mom cry twice in my life, but the setbacks she experienced never affected her faith or relationship with God. She always reassures my siblings and self that, "God never leaves or forsakes us. If He got us through one thing, He will get us through the next thing." She wore Hebrews 13:5 on her face, in her mind, in her prayer closet, and she spoke it. I've seen Jesus Christ's miraculous manifestation in my family's life. My mother continues to be the spiritual pillar to me, and many others. I don't think she knows how many people have been impacted by her noble character and pioneering legacy. She is, and continues to be, a solid rock. Her foundation is built on her testimony that God is a keeper if you want to be kept.

More women of God have crossed my path and taught me the importance of representing my Heavenly Father. They instilled wisdom in me, and inspired me to be a positive role model. I can truly say I've grown over the years, but it was due to good and bad times. The encouragement from women of God who blessed me with a wealth of knowledge has helped me sustain my relationship with Christ. God has never left me, nor forsaken me, and neither will He leave or forsake you. He's our reason for getting up every day. I know folks tell us you get up because of a goal, but our ultimate goal is to please God and we should never leave home without

Him. I can't see life without Jesus Christ. I would have given up a long time ago.

If you're discouraged about being a First Lady, marriage, children, job, bills, or anything that's distracting you from your relationship with the Lord, tell that mountain to GO in JESUS' NAME! You must say it like you mean IT! You were created in the image of God. Woman, even man, is the Bride of Christ. A bride looks forward to being with the bridegroom. As the wedding day approaches, the bride's anticipation is anxious, excited and all thoughts are focused on the happily ever after. The bride is dependent on her husband, which makes him feel complete. She doesn't trust in another, but only leans and depends on him. Who better to fit the shoes of the perfect husband than JESUS CHRIST?

SARAH *vs.* HAGAR

The First Lady constantly faces challenges with family, people, circumstances, friends, jobs, and the church. Her life usually ends up being a constant social media. She faces the paparazzi, church most wanted, spiritual detectives lurking in and out of her life, and those coveting to be her. Be reminded people want the glitz and glamour, but are not willing to pay the price for it.

Abraham was a mighty leader whom God called His friend. He was loyal and loved spending time with the Lord. He had great faith and believed all things were possible. In his life, he experienced a lack of faith.

His wife was barren and she was saddened she couldn't produce children for her husband. She believed in God, but she didn't trust Him. She proved that when she forgot about the promise God told her that she would be a mother of many nations.

If God told me I was going to have a baby at ninety years old, I would hurry up and get my tubes tied. Because of her age, Sarah's faith began to weaken and soon she took matters into her own hands. Sarah told her husband to have a baby with Hagar, her handmaiden. Abraham didn't argue, get upset, struggle, pray, or fast. He went right on in and Hagar got pregnant.

Ladies, can you imagine telling your husband to go have a baby with your housekeeper, who is cuter than you? Do you think you would hear a rebuttal?

Hagar was not happy being the surrogate mother for her mistress. Hagar was upset and she didn't hide it. She started being sarcastic, flaunting her pregnancy in Sarah's face, rubbing her stomach in front of her and, because she was having her mistress' child, she had servants to tend to her.

Sarah vs. Hagar

Sarah knew she made a mistake and should have been patient and waited on the Lord. Unfortunately, it was too late and Hagar was near delivery and on Sarah's last nerve. She got tired of looking at Hagar and told Abraham to send her away. Abraham didn't agree, but God told him to do it to bring peace to the household. When Hagar's child grew to be a boy, she and her child were put out of Abraham's camp.

Hagar was now an outcast, alone and rejected with no place to go. She was in the desert, called on the Lord and the Lord heard her cry. He took care of her and her seed became a great nation.

Sarah eventually got pregnant, had a son, and she, too, became the mother of many nations.

Unfortunately, Hagar's and Sarah's children became lifetime enemies and are fighting to this day—Israel and Iran.

One woman affected nations because she decided to make the wrong choice without God. How many lives affected? How many deaths? How much hate birthed?

A newborn Christian gets saved, and you have the opportunity to plant seeds of encouragement, life, joy, support, and love. Instead, this newborn is greeted with hate, discord, lies, and jealousy. This person spreads that to the next person because of a bad experience and now this seed has cultivated into many seeds.

Ladies, our positions are important and we should not take them lightly. We impact either good or bad. All decisions should include God. Making decisions without Him is wrong. We can unleash many bad things because we didn't take the time to pray and ask for direction.

Do not make decisions based on how you feel. Seek spiritual leadership, be accountable to your spiritual leadership, and allow them to help you make the right decisions. *In the multitude of counselors there is safety* (Proverbs 15:22).

Abraham was the head of the house, he should've said NO! He didn't and both had to experience backlash from the wrong decision. This not only affected them, but generations after them. The power of unbelief can kill, steal, and destroy. If you're struggling to believe

God for something, remember what he has done for you already. If you're reading this book, you are blessed to have the eyes to read. The breath you're breathing is a blessing because you have the opportunity to tell someone about Jesus. You can make a choice to do something that will positively impact the world and generations to come. Include God, include God, include God in every decision.

Sarah caused generational abuse because she stepped ahead of God. Many believers do the same. First Ladies must help their husbands with major decisions and must be careful about the outcome and backlash. Decisions must be birthed through prayer and fasting. Do not make decisions based on emotions. Emotions will cause a lifetime of pain and suffering. Seek godly counsel when you can't reason and, above all, TRUST GOD!

Pastor David W. Cross always says, "You can choose what you want to do, but you can't choose your consequences. Your final decision could be your last; *include God in everything you do!*"

CONCLUSION

Be careful what seeds you plant, remembering they may grow up and be you. What you do today will affect the now, tomorrow, and years to come. The First Lady plants seeds of faith, lives a life of honor, and speaks words of life.

Be God-driven, God-motivated, and God-conscious. Deuteronomy 6:4-9 says, *Love the Lord with all your heart, all your soul, and all your mind.*

All means *all*! Half your mind or soul will leave the other parts vulnerable and as prey for the devil. Love is the motivation to win, succeed, and overcome!

Ladies, strive for excellence. The Proverbs 31 Woman consumed herself with God and Family. Because she put them first, God prospered her business. Pursue a better relationship with God and family. Don't take today for granted because tomorrow is not promised.

References

- The Bible: King James Version (KJV) and New Living Translation (NLT)

- Wikipedia (www.wikipedia.com)

- *Meriam-Webster* (www.webster.com)

About the Author

Yolanda C. Gilliam was born and raised in Los Angeles, California. Her love for writing has always been the pinnacle point of who she is. At an early age, she began writing poems, books, and a host of plays. She published her first work, *Don't Let the Church Steal Your Family* in 2007. Her goal is to impact lives and gain a closer relationship with Jesus Christ. She loves the Lord, her family, and work.

www.ingramcontent.com/pod-product-compliance
Lightning Source LLC
Chambersburg PA
CBHW021136300426
44113CB00006B/453